THE
DRINKER'S
BIBLE

NICHOLAS ANDRE COZZETTO

DISCLAIMER

The Drinker's Bible is intended for audiences
of legal drinking age.

The author, publisher, their agents, officers,
employees, wholesalers, distributors, retailers,
and/or any other persons associated with this
book do not advocate the abuse or misuse of
alcoholic beverages and urge anyone using
the recipes contained herein, do so with
moderation and extreme caution.

The material in this book is for entertainment
purposes. Please consult with your local, state and
federal laws/regulations prior to executing any
of the recipes in this book. By reviewing the
material in this book, you agree to hold
harmless the author, publisher, their agents,
officers, employees, wholesalers, distributors and
retailers from any and all liability or claim that may
arise due to the direct or indirect use of the material
within or any variation there-of.

Never Drink and Drive!

INTRODUCTION

Welcome to The Drinker's Bible: Shots! Shots! Shots!. This book has over 200 of the most essential shooters for making your night the most fun it can be.. A shooter is simply a shot of two or more mixed spirits and usually a non-alcoholic ingredient. Everyone loves a good shooter and now, with this book, you will be a pro and know them all. Be the delight of the party with all the best recipes out there. The shooter today has become commonplace in the bar and club scene, but nobody really knows how to make them and has to pay insane prices to get them. With this book and just a few supplies anyone can make the same professional drinks at home for a mere fraction of the price! After only maybe five shots made on your own, instead of paid for at the bar, this book will have paid for itself. The amount saved, and fun had are limitless with The Drinker's Bible! So enjoy the book and, as always, party safely and have a sober driver.

To get any of the supplies you need to make your party the best it can be, just go to

ShotSkisBarSupplies.com!

Shotski's Bar Supplies is owned by Sunshine Group, LLC, which has been a family run company since day one, and serving all levels of customers with their bar supply needs from the buyer at home, Bars, Clubs, Casino's to large national and international chains and all types of Distributors.

Shotski's Bar Supplies currently offers a wide variety of Bar Supplies designed for economical ways of getting ad-on sales, creating add-on profits and stocking up the Home bar without breaking the bank.

Shotski's has everything, including Shot Glasses, Neon Glow Trays, Lighted Bar Supplies, Glow Sticks, Beer Yards, Test Tubes, Jell-O Injectors, Jager Bomb Shot Cups, Beer Pong Tables and so much more.

So scan the QR code below to get your party started the right way with Shotski's!

TABLE OF
CONTENTS

GIN

Alabama Slammer (gin)

- ½ oz amaretto almond liqueur
- ½ oz peach liqueur
- ½ oz sloe gin
- Splash of orange juice
- Splash of sweet and sour

Shake the ingredients over ice, strain into a shot glass, and serve.

Areola

- 1 oz peach schnapps
- ½ oz Canadian whiskey
- ½ oz sloe gin

Pour the ingredients in the above order into a shot glass and serve.

Angel's Delight

- 1 oz gin
- 1 oz triple sec
- Dash cream liqueur

Shake over ice, strain into shot glass, and serve.

B L A C K O U T

- ½ oz gin
- ½ oz blackberry brandy
- ¼ oz lime juice
- ¼ oz sugar syrup

Shake ingredients, strain, and serve.

B U L L   S H I T

- 1 oz Hypnotiq liqueur
- 1 oz Red Bull
- 1 oz sloe gin

Mix ingredients in a shaker with ice, pour into a large shot glass, and serve.

B U L L   S W E A T

- 1 oz sloe gin
- Dash of tabasco sauce

Pour the gin in a shot glass, add a dash of Tabasco, and serve.

CABIN 21

- 1 oz Canadian whiskey
- ½ oz black sambuca
- 1 splash gin

Pour in the above order into a shot glass and serve.

CRANK HEAD

- ½ oz white sambuca
- ½ oz Irish cream
- ½ oz gin
- 1 splash of grenadine

Float the ingredients in the above order carefully, splash the grenadine in the center, and serve.

EARTHQUAKE

- 1/3 oz Canadian whiskey
- 1/3 oz anise liqueur
- 1/3 oz gin

Shake the ingredients over ice, strain into shot glass, and serve.

EMERALD EYE

- ½ oz gin
- ½ oz melon liqueur
- ½ oz Blue Curacao

Pour in the above order and serve.

EVIL TONGUE

- 1 ½ oz gin
- 1 oz melon liqueur
- 1 splash sweet and sour
- 1 splash 7-Up

Shake ingredients over ice, strain, and serve.

GLOWSTICK

- ¾ oz gin
- ¾ oz melon liqueur
- 1 splash sweet and sour

Mix in a shaker with ice, strain into a shot glass, and serve.

I T A L I A N V A L I U M

- 1 oz amaretto liqueur
- ½ oz gin

Mix the ingredients in a shot glass and serve.

M A C H 1

- 1 oz sloe gin
- 1 oz 7-Up

Pour into a large shot glass and serve.

M O N E Y S H O T

- ½ oz sloe gin
- ½ oz advocaat liqueur
- ½ oz cherry brandy

Layer in the above order and serve.

P A M O Y O

- 1 oz gin
- ¾ oz lemonade
- ¾ oz grape juice

Shake ingredients over ice, strain into shot glass, and serve.

P A R A D I S E

- ½ oz apricot brandy
- ½ oz orange juice
- ½ oz gin

Shake the ingredients over ice, strain into shot glasses, and serve.

P I C K L E D   P L A C E N T A

- ½ oz Irish cream
- ½ oz vermouth
- ½ oz gin

Layer in the above order and serve.

PLEAD THE FIFTH

- ½ oz gin
- ½ oz sambuca
- ½ oz coffee liqueur

Mix the ingredients over ice, strain, and serve.

SILVER BULLET

- 1 ¼ oz gin
- ¾ oz scotch
- lemon twist

Shake the ingredients over ice and strain into shot glass. Squeeze the lemon twist over the shot, garnish with it, and serve.

YELLOW HAZE

- ½ oz Bacardi Limon rum
- ½ oz gin
- ½ oz Mountain Dew
- 1 splash lime juice

Mix the rum and gin, add a splash of lime juice, then top off with Mountain Dew and serve.

LIQUEURS

After Five

- ½ oz coffee liqueur
- ½ oz Irish cream liqueur
- ½ oz peppermint schnapps

Layer in the above order in a shot glass and serve.

Alabama Slammer

- 1 oz amaretto almond liqueur
- 1 oz whiskey
- 1 oz OJ
- 1 oz crème de noyaux

Shake everything over ice, strain into shot glasses, and serve.

Apocalypse Now

- 1/3 oz dry vermouth
- 1/3 oz Irish cream liqueur
- 1/3 oz tequila

Pour the ingredients into a shot glass and serve.

A T T I T U D E A D J U S T M E N T

- ½ oz Irish cream
- ½ oz root beer schnapps
- ½ oz peach liqueur

Layer in the above order in a shot glass and serve.

B - 5 1

- ½ oz coffee liqueur
- ½ oz Irish cream
- ½ oz hazelnut liqueur

Layer in the above order in a shot glass and serve.

B - 5 2

- ½ oz orange liqueur
- ½ oz chocolate liqueur
- ½ oz Irish cream

Shake the ingredients over ice, strain, and serve.

B - 5 3

- ½ oz coffee liqueur
- ½ oz sambuca
- ½ oz orange liqueur

Layer in the above order in a shot glass and serve.

BANANA CREAM PIE

- ½ oz coffee liqueur
- ½ oz Licor 43 liqueur
- ½ oz banana schnapps

Layer in the above order in a shot glass and serve.

BAZOOKA JOE

- ½ oz Irish cream liqueur
- ½ oz banana liqueur
- ½ oz blue curacao liqueur

Shake the ingredients over ice, strain into shot glass, and serve.

B E A M M E U P S C O T T Y

- ½ oz coffee liqueur
- ½ oz crème de banana
- ½ oz Irish cream liqueur

Shake the ingredients over ice, strain into a shot glass, and serve.

B L O O D C L O T

- 1 ½ oz Southern Comfort peach liqueur
- ¾ oz grenadine
- 7-Up

Pour the grenadine and 7-Up into a lowball glass, drop in the Southern Comfort shot, and slam!

B L O W J O B

- ½ oz Irish cream
- 1 oz amaretto almond liqueur
- Whipped cream

Pour the ingredients into the shot glass. Top it off with whipped cream and enjoy, but your not supposed to use your hands to drink!

BLUE SMURFF PISS

- ½ oz Jagermeister
- ½ oz 151 rum
- ½ oz peppermint liqueur
- ½ oz blue curacao liqueur

Pour as listed. Strain through ice into shot glasses and serve.

BRAIN ERASER

- 1 oz cinnamon schnapps
- 1 oz coffee liqueur
- 1 oz vodka

Layer in the above order in a large shot glass keeping everything separate. Slide a straw down the side of the glass carefully and suck from the bottom quickly! For a normal size shot just halve everything.

BROKEN DOWN GOLF CART

- 1 oz amaretto almond liqueur
- 1 oz melon liqueur
- Dash of lime juice

Shake all of the above and strain though ice into a shot glass.

BULL SHIT

- ½ oz Hypnotiq liqueur
- ½ oz Red Bull
- ½ oz sloe gin

Mix ingredients in a shaker with ice, pour into a shot glass, and serve.

BUMBLE BEE

- ½ oz Irish cream
- ½ oz coffee liqueur
- ½ oz sambuca

Layer in the above order very carefully and it should resemble a bumble bee.

BURNING NAZI

- ½ oz Jagermeister
- ½ oz peppermint liqueur

Serve chilled or mix over ice and strain into a shot glass.

BUTTERBALL

- 1 oz amaretto almond liqueur
- 1 oz butterscotch schnapps

Layer in the above order in a shot glass and add whipped cream for fun.

BUTTERY NIPPLE

- 1 oz DeKuyper ButterShots liqueur
- ½ oz Irish cream

Using a chilled shot glass layer in the above order and serve.

BUTTERY NIPPLE WITH A CHERRY KISS

- ¾ oz butterscotch schnapps
- ¾ oz Irish cream
- 1 tsp cherry liqueur
- 1 cherry

Layer in the above order in a shot glass with the schnapps and Irish cream. Then add a tsp of cherry liqueur to the top of the shot with a cherry in the spoon.

C A N D Y   C O R N

- 1/3 oz Licor 43 liqueur
- 1/3 oz orange curacao liqueur
- 1/3 oz cream

Layer in the above order carefully and it should resemble the halloween candy!

C E M E N T   M I X E R

- 1 shot Irish cream
- 1 shot lime juice

Hold the shot of Irish cream in your mouth, then add the lime juice. Mix thoroughly in your mouth and consume.

C H I N A   W H I T E

- ½ oz vodka
- ½ oz Irish cream
- ½ oz white crème de cacao

Shake everything over ice and strain into shot glasses.

CHOCOLATE CAKE

- ¾ oz citrus vodka
- ¾ oz hazelnut liqueur
- 1 lemon wedge

Mix in a shot glass and serve. Follow by sucking on a sugar-coated lemon wedge.

CHOCOLATE COATED CHERRY

- ½ oz coffee liqueur
- ½ oz amaretto
- ½ oz light crème de cacao
- grenadine

Pour the ingredients into a shaker. Shake then strain into a shot glass. Place a drop of grenadine in the center of the shot and serve.

CHOCOLATE COVERED CHERRY

- ½ oz coffee liqueur
- ½ oz Irish Cream
- ¼ oz grenadine

Shake the ingredients over ice, strain and serve.

Comfort Zone

- ½ oz Southern Comfort
- ½ oz amaretto
- ½ oz pineapple juice

Shake the ingredients, strain, and serve.

Cowboy Cocksucker

- ½ oz butterscotch schnapps
- ½ oz Irish cream

Mix in a shot glass and serve.

Cucacaracha

- 1/3 oz vodka
- 1/3 oz coffee liqueur
- 1/3 oz tequila
- Club soda

Mix in a shot glass, top with the club soda, and serve.

CUM SCORCHER

- 1/3 oz butterscotch schnapps
- 1/3 oz vodka
- 1/3 oz coffee liqueur
- Dash of Irish cream

Pour into a shot glass in the above order, slowly add the Irish cream last, and serve.

CUM SHOT

- ½ oz butterscotch schnapps
- ½ oz Irish cream
- Whipped cream

Mix the above in a shot glass, top with whipped cream, and serve.

CURTAIN CALL

- ½ oz Jagermeister
- ½ oz melon liqueur
- ½ oz whiskey

Shake the ingredients over ice, strain into shot glass, and serve.

D E A D N A Z I

- 2/3 oz peppermint liqueur
- 2/3 oz Jagermeister

Pour into a shot glass, chilled, in the above order, and serve.

D I R T Y N I P P L E

- 1/3 oz coffee liqueur
- 1/3 oz sambuca
- 1/3 oz Irish cream

Layer in the above order and serve.

D I R T Y O A T M E A L

- 1 ½ oz Jagermeister
- 1 ½ oz Irish cream

Layer in the above order and serve.

D U C K   F A R T

- ½ oz whiskey
- ½ oz amaretto almond liqueur
- ½ oz Irish cream

Layer in the above order and serve.

F I R E   A N D   I C E

- ¾ oz 151 rum
- ¾ oz peppermint liqueur

Pour the ingredients into a shot glass and serve.

F L A M I N G   D O C T O R   P E P P E R

- Draft beer
- ¼ oz 151 rum
- ¾ oz amaretto almond liqueur

Fill a mug with half of a beer. Pour amaretto into the shot glass and float the 151 on the top. Light the 151 on fire, drop into the mug, and chug! Make sure the fire is completely extinguished before drinking.

FOREPLAY

- ½ oz amaretto
- ½ oz pineapple juice

Pour the ingredients into a shaker with ice. Shake, strain, and serve.

FRENCH TICKLER

- 1 oz cinnamon schnapps
- ½ oz orange liqueur

Shake the ingredients, strain, and serve.

FUNKY BITCH

- ½ oz coffee liqueur
- ½ oz vodka
- ½ oz Irish Cream
- ½ oz hazelnut liqueur

Shake the ingredients, strain, and serve.

GLADIATOR

- ½ oz amaretto
- ½ oz Southern Comfort
- 7 Up
- Orange juice

This is a drop shot. Pour the liqueurs into a shot glass. Pour the 7 Up and orange juice into a glass. Drop the shot into the glass and drink.

GLOWSTICK

- ¾ oz gin
- ¾ oz melon liqueur
- 1 splash sweet and sour

Mix in a shaker with ice, strain into a shot glass, and serve.

GOLD BARON

- ¾ oz peppermint liqueur
- ¼ oz cinnamon schnapps

Layer in the above order and serve.

GOLDEN NIPPLE

- ½ oz cinnamon schnapps
- ½ oz butterscotch schnapps
- Irish cream

Pour in the cinnamon and butterscotch schnapps, top off shot glass with Irish cream, and serve.

GREEN MOTHERFUCKER

- ½ oz 151 rum
- ½ oz green crème de menthe

Pour into a shot glass and serve.

HAND GRENADE

- ½ oz Jagermeister
- ½ oz peppermint schnapps
- ½ oz 151 rum

Shake the ingredients over ice, strain into shot glass, and serve.

HOOTER

- ¾ oz vodka
- ¾ oz amaretto

Pour the ingredients into a shot glass and serve.

HOT APPLE PIE

- ½ oz Irish cream
- ½ oz cinnamon schnapps
- Dash cinnamon

Mix the above into a shot glass and sprinkle cinnamon on the top. Light the cinnamon with a match. Blow out the flame and shoot.

ICE BREAKER

- ¾ oz peppermint liqueur
- ¾ oz Yukon Jack

Pour the ingredients into a shot glass and serve.

IRISH CAR BOMB

- ¾ pint Guinness
- ¾ oz Irish whiskey
- ¾ oz Irish cream

Pour the Irish cream in the shot glass and layer the whiskey on top. Pour the Guinness in a pint glass. Drop the shot into the pint glass and chug!

ITALIAN VALIUM

- 2/3 oz amaretto liqueur
- 1/3 oz gin

Mix the ingredients in a shot glass and serve.

JAGER BOMB

- 1 shot Jagermeister
- 1/3 can Red Bull

Fill a glass with 1/3 of a can of Red Bull. Pour a shot of Jagermeister, drop it into the Red Bull, and chug.

JELLY BEAN

- ½ oz blackberry brandy or grenadine
- ½ oz anisette or sambuca
- ½ oz Southern Comfort

Pour the brandy or grenadine into the shot glass. Layer the anisette or sambuca on top carefully. Layer the Southern Comfort on top of that and serve.

JENNIFER'S ORGASM

- ¾ oz Dekuyper Buttershots liqueur
- ¾ oz spiced rum

Shake the ingredients over ice, strain into shot glasses, and serve.

KAMIKAZE

- ½ oz tequila½ oz triple sec
- ½ oz lime juice

Pour into a shot glass and serve.

KOOL AID

- ½ oz melon liqueur
- ½ oz amaretto
- Cranberry juice

Pour the melon liqueur and amaretto into the shot glass. Top off with cranberry juice and serve.

LADY GODIVA

- ½ oz orange liqueur
- ½ oz coffee liqueur
- ½ oz cream

Shake the ingredients, strain, and serve.

LEG SPREADER

- ¾ oz coffee liqueur
- ¾ oz Galliano liqueur

Shake the ingredients, strain, and serve.

LEMON SHOT

- ½ oz Galliano liqueur
- ½ oz citrus vodka
- 151 rum
- Sugar
- 1 lemon wedge

Mix the vodka and Galliano in the shot glass. Sprinkle sugar on the lemon wedge and place it on the shot glass. Pour 151 on the lemon wedge and glass. Light, let it burn for a moment, and blow it out. Take the shot and bite the lemon.

LIQUID ASPHALT

- ¾ oz sambuca
- ¾ oz Jagermeister

Chill the ingredients, layer in the above order, and serve.

L I Q U I D C O C A I N E

- ¼ oz orange liqueur
- ¼ oz peach liqueur
- ¼ oz vodka
- ¼ oz amaretto almond liqueur
- Splash pineapple juice

Shake everything over ice, strain, and serve in shot glasses.

L I Q U I D C R A C K

- 1/3 oz peppermint liqueur
- 1/3 oz Jagermeister
- 1/3 oz cinnamon schnapps

Mix all of the ingredients in a shot glass and serve.

L I Q U I D H E R O I N E

- 1 ½ oz peppermint liqueur
- 1 ½ oz Jagermeister

Mix over ice, strain into shot glasses, and serve.

M & M

- ½ oz coffee liqueur
- ½ oz amaretto

Layer in the above order in shot glass and serve.

MAGE'S FIRE

- ½ oz vodka
- ¼ oz cinnamon schnapps
- ¼ oz Blue Curacao liqueur

Mix the ingredients in a bottle, chill for 24 hours, and serve as shots.

MELON BALL

- ¼ oz melon liqueur
- ¼ oz pineapple juice
- ½ oz vodka

Pour the ingredients into a mixing glass with ice. Stir, strain, and serve.

M I D N I G H T O I L

- 1 ½ oz amaretto liqueur
- ½ oz Jagermeister

Mix all of the ingredients in a shot glass and serve.

M O N E Y S H O T

- 1/3 oz sloe gin
- 1/3 oz advocaat liqueur
- 1/3 oz cherry brandy

Layer in the above order and serve.

M O O S E F A R T

- ¼ oz vodka
- ¼ oz Canadian whiskey
- ¼ oz coffee liqueur
- ¼ oz Irish cream

Blend with ice until thick in consistency, pour into shot glasses, and serve.

MOTOR OIL

- 1 oz Jagermeister
- ½ oz peppermint schnapps
- ½ oz cinnamon schnapps
- ½ oz coconut rum

Using a triple shot glass, pour the ingredients in the order above and serve.

NAZI HELMET

- ½ oz Jagermeister liqueur
- ½ oz peppermint liqueur

Mix the ingredients in a shot glass and serve.

NAZI SURFER

- ½ oz Jagermeister liqueur
- ½ oz coconut rum
- ½ oz melon liqueur
- Splash pineapple juice
- Dash grenadine syrup

Shake all of the ingredients over ice, strain into shot glasses, and serve.

NAZI TACO

- ½ oz Jagermeister liqueur
- ½ oz tequila
- 1/3 oz Tabasco sauce

Mix all of the ingredients in a shot glass and serve.

NUTS 'N BERRIES

- 2/3 oz lemon vodka
- 1/3 oz hazelnut liqueur
- 2/3 oz cranberry juice

Mix all of the ingredients and chill. After chilled, strain into shot glasses and serve.

NUTTY IRISHMAN

- ¾ oz Irish cream
- ¾ oz hazelnut liqueur

Pour the ingredients into a shot glass and serve.

O A T M E A L   C O O K I E

- ½ oz orange liqueur
- ½ oz butterscotch schnapps
- ½ oz Irish cream

Shake all of the ingredients over ice, strain into shot glasses, and serve.

O I L   S L I C K

- ½ oz white crème de menthe
- ½ oz black sambuca

Layer the ingredients in the above order carefully and shoot.

O I L   S P I L L

- ¾ oz cinnamon schnapps
- ¼ oz Jagermeister liqueur

Layer the ingredients in the above order carefully and shoot.

O R G A S M

- ½ oz peppermint schnapps
- ½ oz Irish cream

Pour the ingredients into the shot glass and serve.

P A N T Y   B U R N E R

- ½ oz amaretto
- ½ oz coffee liqueur
- ½ oz hazelnut liqueur

Stir the ingredients in a glass and serve.

P E A N U T   B U T T E R   A N D   J E L L Y

- ¾ oz hazelnut liqueur
- ¾ oz Chambord liqueur

Pour the ingredients into a shaker with ice. Shake, strain, and serve.

PEARL NECKLACE

- ½ oz Tequila Rose strawberry cream liqueur
- ½ oz Irish cream

Mix the ingredients in the shot glass and serve.

PIERCED NIPPLE

- ½ oz sambuca
- ½ oz Irish cream

Shake the ingredients over ice, strain into shot glasses, and serve.

PICKLED PLACENTA

- 1/3 oz Irish cream
- 1/3 oz vermouth
- 1/3 oz gin

Layer in the above order and serve.

P I N K N I P P L E

- ¾ oz raspberry liqueur
- ¾ oz Bailey's Irish Cream

Shake the ingredients and strain into a shot glass. Place a drop of grenadine in the center of the shot and serve.

P I R A T E ' S T R E A S U R E

- ¾ cinnamon schnapps
- ¾ oz spiced rum

Carefully layer in the above order and serve.

P I T B U L L O N C R A C K

- ¼ oz tequila
- ¼ oz Jagermeister
- ¼ oz bourbon whiskey
- ¼ oz 151 rum

Chill the ingredients, combine in a shot glass, and serve.

PLEAD THE FIFTH

- 1/3 oz gin
- 1/3 oz sambuca
- 1/3 oz coffee liqueur

Mix the ingredients over ice, strain, and serve.

POLAR BEAR

- ½ oz crème de cacao
- ½ oz peppermint schnapps

Shake the ingredients over ice, strain into shot glasses, and serve.

PURPLE HAZE

- ½ oz sambuca
- ½ oz raspberry liqueur

Layer the ingredients in the order above carefully and serve.

PURPLE HOOTER

- ½ oz vodka
- ½ oz raspberry liqueur
- Splash 7-Up soda

Shake the ingredients over ice, strain into shot glasses, and serve.

QUICKIE

- ½ oz blackberry brandy
- ½ oz crème de banana
- ½ oz Irish Cream

Shake the ingredients, strain, and serve.

RATTLESNAKE

- 1/3 oz Irish cream
- 1/3 oz coffee liqueur
- 1/3 oz crème de cacao

Layer the ingredients in the order above carefully and serve.

RED BARON

- ¾ oz peppermint liqueur
- ¼ oz cinnamon schnapps

Layer the ingredients in the above order carefully and serve.

RED ROYAL

- 1 ½ oz Canadian whiskey
- ½ oz amaretto almond liqueur

Pour the ingredients into the shot glass in the above order and serve.

RED SNAPPER

- 1 oz Canadian whiskey
- 1 oz amaretto liqueur
- 2 oz cranberry juice

Pour into a shaker with ice. Shake, strain into shot glasses, and serve.

RED, WHITE, AND BLUE

- 1/3 oz grenadine
- 1/3 oz peach schnapps
- 1/3 oz blue curacao

Layer the ingredients very carefully in the above order and serve.

REDHEAD'S NIPPLE

- 1 oz vanilla schnapps
- 1 oz Irish cream

Layer the ingredients in the above order carefully and serve.

REDHEADED SLUT

- 1 oz Jagermeister
- 1 oz peach schnapps
- 2 oz cranberry juice

Pour the ingredients into a shaker with ice. Shake, strain, and serve.

REDNECK PRAIRE FIRE

- 1 oz White Lightning cider
- 1/8 oz Louisiana hot sauce

Layer the ingredients in the above order carefully, wait until the hot sauce seeps down a bit, and shoot.

ROASTED TOASTY

- ½ oz cinnamon schnapps
- ½ oz amaretto
- ½ oz coffee liqueur

Shake the ingredients over ice, strain into shot glass, and serve.

ROCKY MOUNTAIN BEAR FUCK

- 1 oz blue curacao liqueur
- 1 oz melon liqueur
- 2 splashes Canadian Club whiskey

Shake the Blue Curacao and melon liqueur over ice and strain into shot glasses. Top off the shot with 2 splashes of the Canadian whiskey and serve.

RUSSIAN QUAALUDE

- 2/3 oz hazelnut liqueur
- 2/3 oz Irish cream liqueur
- 2/3 oz vodka

Layer the ingredients in the above order and serve.

SANTA SHOT

- ½ oz grenadine
- ½ oz green crème de menthe
- ½ oz peppermint schnapps

Layer the ingredients in the above order carefully and serve.

SCREAMING NAZI

- 1 oz Jagermeister
- 1 oz peppermint liqueur

Shake the ingredients over ice, strain into shot glasses, and serve.

S E X   O N   T H E   B E A C H

- 1 oz vodka
- 1 oz triple sec
- 1 oz apple schnapps
- 1 oz peach schnapps
- 1 oz Southern Comfort peach liqueur
- 2 ½ oz OJ
- 2 ½ oz 7-Up soda
- 1 tbsp grenadine syrup

Mix all of the ingredients in a pitcher of ice. Strain into a bottle and serve as shots.

S H I T   O N   T H E   G R A S S

- 1 oz melon liqueur
- 1 oz coffee liqueur

Layer the ingredients in the above order and serve.

S I L V E R   N I P P L E

- 1 oz Sambuca
- 1 oz vodka

Stir the ingredients in a glass, strain, and serve.

S I T O N M Y F A C E

- 2/3 oz coffee liqueur
- 2/3 oz hazelnut liqueur
- 2/3 oz Irish cream

Layer the ingredients in the above order and serve.

S L I P P E R Y N I P P L E

- 1 oz sambuca
- ½ oz Irish Cream
- Grenadine

Layer the ingredients in the order above in a shot glass. Place a drop of grenadine in the center and serve.

S M U R F F A R T

- ½ oz blue curacao liqueur
- 1 oz blueberry schnapps
- Splash of cream

Shake over ice, strain into shot glasses, and serve.

SMURF ON THE RAG

- ½ oz peach schnapps
- ½ oz Blue Curacao liqueur
- 1 ½ oz whipped cream
- Couple drops grenadine syrup

Mix the schnapps and Blue Curacao in the shot glass. Top with whipped cream, add a couple drops of grenadine on top, and serve.

SMURF PISS

- 1 oz blue curacao liqueur
- 1 oz Black Haus blackberry schnapps
- Splash pineapple juice
- Splash Sprite soda

Chill the ingredients, mix in a shot glass, and serve.

SNAKE BITE

- ½ oz Green Chartreuse
- ½ oz vodka
- 2 drops Tabasco sauce

Layer the ingredients carefully in the above order. Drop the Tabasco in so that the drops go to the bottom of the shot and serve.

SNOWBALL

- ¾ oz brandy
- ¾ oz peppermint schnapps
- ¾ oz white crème de cacao

Shake the ingredients over ice, strain into shot glasses, and serve.

SOUTHERN BLUES

- ½ oz Southern Comfort peach liqueur
- ½ oz blueberry schnapps

Shake over ice, strain into a shot glass, and serve.

SOUTHERN BRAIN DAMAGE

- 2/3 oz Southern Comfort peach liqueur
- 1/3 oz Tia Maria coffee liqueur
- Couple drops grenadine syrup

Layer the ingredients in the above order carefully, add a couple drops of grenadine, and serve.

SQUISHED SMURF

- ½ oz peach schnapps
- ¼ oz Irish cream
- ¼ oz blue curacao liqueur
- Couple drops grenadine syrup

Layer the Bailey's on top of the peach schnapps. Dribble Blue Curacao over the top and it will curdle around the Bailey's. Drop in some grenadine around the shot glass and serve.

Sweet and Tangy

- ¾ oz Southern Comfort
- ¾ oz melon liqueur
- ½ oz sweet and sour mix

Shake the ingredients, strain, and serve.

T-52

- ½ oz coffee liqueur
- ½ oz Tequila Rose strawberry cream liqueur
- ½ oz orange liqueur

Layer the ingredients in the above order and serve.

Toastie

- 1 ¼ oz amaretto
- 1/3 oz cinnamon schnapps

Pour the ingredients into a shot glass in the above order and serve.

Tootsie Roll

- 1/3 oz Tia Maria coffee liqueur
- 1/3 oz dark crème de cacao
- 1/3 oz hazelnut liqueur

Pour the ingredients into a shot glass and serve.

Urine Sample

- ½ oz Galliano herbal liqueur
- ½ oz sambuca

Pour the ingredients into a shot glass and serve.

Watermelon

- 1 oz vodka
- 1 oz amaretto almond liqueur
- 1 oz Southern Comfort peach liqueur
- 1 oz OJ
- 1 oz pineapple juice
- Dash of grenadine syrup

Shake the ingredients over ice, strain into shot glasses, and serve.

WOLF BITE

- 1 oz absinthe
- 1 oz melon liqueur
- Splash lemon-lime soda
- 1 ½ oz pineapple juice
- Drizzle of grenadine

Shake the absinthe, melon liqueur, and pineapple juice over ice and strain into a large shot glass. Splash lemon-lime soda on top, followed by a drizzle of grenadine. Serve.

Y2K

- ½ oz coffee liqueur
- ¾ oz Canadian whiskey

Mix in a chilled shot glass and serve.

RUM

AFTERBURNER

- ¾ oz Aftershock Hot & Cool cinnamon schnapps
- ¾ oz 151 rum

Pour both ingredients into the shot glass, let mix, and serve.

BIG BAMBOO

- 2 oz 151 proof rum
- 1 oz dark rum
- ¼ oz triple sec
- 2 oz orange juice
- 2 oz pineapple juice
- ½ oz simple syrup
- dash of bitters

This will make 3 to 4 shots! Shake all ingredients over ice, strain into shot glasses, and serve.

DEATH ROW

- ¾ oz whiskey
- ¾ oz 151 rum

Shake the ingredients over ice, strain into shot glass, and serve.

F I R E A N D I C E

- ¾ oz 151 rum
- ¾ oz peppermint schnapps

  Pour the ingredients into a shot glass and serve.

F I R E I N H E A V E N

- 1 shot 151 rum
- Dash Tabasco sauce

  Fill the shot with the rum, add a dash of Tabasco, and serve.

F I R E B A L L 2

- ¾ oz white rum
- ¾ oz schnapps
- 2 dashes Tabasco sauce

  Shake the ingredients over ice, strain into shot glass, and serve.

FLAMING DOCTOR PEPPER

- Draft beer
- ¼ oz 151 rum
- ¾ oz amaretto almond liqueur

Fill a mug with half of a beer. Pour amaretto into the shot glass and float the 151 on the top. Light the 151 on fire, drop into the mug, and chug!

GORILLA FART

- ½ oz 151 rum
- ½ oz bourbon whiskey

Pour into a shot glass and serve.

GREEN MOTHERFUCKER

- ½ oz 151 rum
- ½ oz green crème de menthe

Pour into a shot glass and serve.

H A N D G R E N A D E

- ½ oz Jagermeister
- ½ oz peppermint schnapps
- ½ oz 151 rum

Shake the ingredients over ice, strain into shot glass, and serve.

H O R N Y B U L L

- ½ shot 1800 Tequila
- ½ shot rum

Pour into a shot glass and serve.

J E N N I F E R ' S O R G A S M

- ¾ oz Dekuyper Buttershots liqueur
- ¾ oz spiced rum

Shake over ice, strain into shot glasses, and serve.

LIQUID STEAK

- 1 shot 151 rum
- Dash of Worcestershire sauce

Pour a shot of Bacardi 151 rum, add a dash of Worcestershire sauce, and serve.

MOTOR OIL

- 1 oz Jagermeister
- ½ oz peppermint schnapps
- ½ oz cinnamon schnapps
- ½ oz coconut rum

Using a triple shot glass, pour the ingredients in the order above and serve.

NAZI SURFER

- ½ oz Jagermeister
- ½ oz coconut rum
- ½ oz melon liqueur
- Splash pineapple juice
- Dash grenadine syrup

Shake all of the ingredients over ice, strain into shot glasses, and serve.

Nymphomaniac

- 1 oz spiced rum
- ½ oz peach schnapps
- ½ oz coconut rum

Shake the ingredients over ice, strain into shot glass, and serve.

Pirate's Treasure

- ¾ cinnamon schnapps
- ¾ oz spiced rum

Carefully layer in the above order and serve.

Pit Bull on Crack

- 1/3 oz tequila
- 1/3 oz Jagermeister
- 1/3 oz bourbon whiskey
- 1/3 oz 151 rum

Chill the ingredients, combine in a shot glass, and serve.

VOODOO

- ½ oz Tia Maria
- ½ oz rum cream
- ½ oz 151 rum

Layer the ingredients carefully in the above order and serve.

YELLOW HAZE

- ¼ oz lemon rum
- ¼ oz gin
- ½ oz Mountain Dew
- 1 splash lime juice

Mix the rum and gin, add a splash of lime juice, then top off with Mountain Dew and serve.

SCHNAPPS

A F T E R   F I V E

- ½ oz coffee liqueur
- ½ oz Irish cream liqueur
- ½ oz peppermint schnapps

Layer in the above order in a shot glass and serve.

A F T E R B U R N E R

- ¾ oz cinnamon schnapps
- ¾ oz 151 rum

Pour both ingredients into the shot glass, let mix, and serve.

A L I E N   N I P P L E

- ½ oz butterscotch schnapps
- ¼ oz Irish cream
- ¼ oz melon liqueur

Pour in the butterscotch first, then layer the Irish cream, and finish with a layer of the melon liqueur. Serve.

A REOLA

- ½ oz peach schnapps
- ¼ oz Canadian whiskey
- ¼ oz sloe gin

Pour the ingredients in the above order into a shot glass and serve.

A NTI - V ENOM

- 1 oz peppermint schnapps
- ½ oz Irish cream

Layer the ingredients in the order above and serve.

A SS

- ½ oz vodka
- ½ oz spearmint schnapps
- ½ oz sambuca

Pour the ingredients into a shot glass and serve.

BLUE POLAR BEAR

- 1 oz vodka
- 1 oz chilled peppermint schnapps
- Crushed ice

Shake the vodka and peppermint schnapps until mixed. Add in the crushed ice for another light shaking and pour into shot glasses.

BRAIN ERASER

- 1 oz cinnamon schnapps
- 1 oz coffee liqueur
- 1 oz vodka

Layer in the above order in a large shot glass keeping everything separate. Slide a straw down the side of the glass carefully and suck from the bottom quickly!

B R A I N   T U M O R

- 1 oz peach schnapps
- Irish cream
- Grenadine
- Cherry brandy

Fill the shot glass about ¾ of the way with peach schnapps. Layer the Bailey's on the top. Then put a couple drops of grenadine down the middle, followed in the same way by a couple drops of cherry brandy.

B R A N D E D   N I P P L E

- ½ oz butterscotch schnapps
- ½ oz Irish cream
- ½ oz cinnamon schnapps
- Dash of 151 rum

Layer in the above order in a shot glass. Light the 151 on fire and shoot!

BRUSH FIRE

- 1/3 oz Tabasco sauce
- 2/3 oz cinnamon schnapps

Layer in the above order into a shot glass and drink immediately!

BUTTERBALL

- ¾ oz amaretto almond liqueur
- ¾ oz butterscotch schnapps

Layer in the above order in a shot glass and add whipped cream for fun.

BUTTERY NIPPLE WITH A CHERRY KISS

- ½ oz butterscotch schnapps
- ½ oz Irish cream
- 1 tsp cherry liqueur
- 1 cherry

Layer in the above order in a shot glass with the schnapps and Irish cream. Then add a tsp of cherry liqueur to the top of the shot with a cherry in the spoon.

CARMEL APPLE

- ¾ oz apple schnapps
- ¾ oz butterscotch schnapps

Mix together freezer cold in a shot glass and serve.

CARMEL SOUR APPLE

- ½ oz DeKuyper Sour Apple Pucker schnapps
- ½ oz butterscotch schnapps

Shake over ice and serve in shot glasses.

CHERRY CHEESECAKE

- ¾ oz vanilla schnapps
- Cranberry juice

Pour the vanilla schnapps in the shot glass, fill the rest of the way with cranberry juice, and serve.

COWBOY COCKSUCKER

- ½ oz butterscotch schnapps
- ½ oz Irish cream

Mix in a shot glass and serve.

CUM SCORCHER

- 1/3 shot butterscotch schnapps
- 1/3 shot Absolut vodka
- 1/3 shot Kahlua coffee liqueur
- Dash Carolans Irish cream

Pour into a shot glass in the above order, slowly add the Irish cream last, and serve.

CUM SHOT

- ¾ oz butterscotch schnapps
- ¾ oz Irish cream
- Whipped cream

Mix the above in a shot glass, top with whipped cream, and serve.

F IREBALL **1**

- 1 shot cinnamon schnapps
- Dash Tabasco sauce

  Fill the shot with cinnamon schnapps, add a dash of Tabasco, and serve.

F IREBALL **2**

- ¾ oz white rum
- ¾ oz schnapps
- 2 dashes Tabasco sauce

  Shake the ingredients over ice, strain into shot glass, and serve.

F IRECRACKER

- ½ oz tequila
- ½ oz cinnamon schnapps
- ½ oz peppermint schnapps

  Shake the ingredients over ice, strain into shot glass, and serve.

FRENCH TICKLER

- 1 oz cinnamon schnapps
- ½ oz Grand Marnier

Shake the ingredients, strain, and serve.

GOLD BARON

- ¾ oz peppermint liqueur
- ¼ oz cinnamon schnapps

Layer in the above order and serve.

GOLDEN NIPPLE

- ½ oz cinnamon schnapps
- ½ oz butterscotch schnapps
- Irish cream

Pour in the cinnamon and butterscotch schnapps, top off shot glass with Irish cream, and serve.

GOLDSCHLAGER LEMONDROP

- 1 oz Goldschlager cinnamon schnapps
- 2 oz lemonade

Shake with ice, strain into shot glass, and serve.

HAND GRENADE

- ½ oz Jagermeister
- ½ oz peppermint schnapps
- ½ oz 151 rum

Shake the ingredients over ice, strain into shot glass, and serve.

HOT APPLE PIE

- ¾ oz Irish cream
- ¾ oz cinnamon schnapps
- Dash cinnamon

Mix the above into a shot glass and sprinkle cinnamon on the top. Light the cinnamon with a match. Blow out the flame and shoot.

HOT PANTS

- 1 oz peach schnapps
- ½ oz pepper vodka

Pour the ingredients into a shot glass and serve.

IRON CROSS

- ¾ oz peppermint schnapps
- ¾ oz apricot brandy

Shake the ingredients over ice, strain into shot glass, and serve.

LIQUID CRACK

- ½ oz peppermint liqueur
- ½ oz Jagermeister
- ½ oz cinnamon schnapps

Mix all of the ingredients in a shot glass and serve.

MAD SCIENTIST

- ¾ oz blueberry schnapps
- ¾ oz raspberry schnapps
- Grenadine syrup
- Irish cream

Pour both schnapps in a shot glass. Top off with grenadine and a splash of Bailey's and serve.

MAGE'S FIRE

- 1 oz vodka
- ½ oz cinnamon schnapps
- ½ oz blue curacao liqueur

Mix the ingredients in a bottle, chill for 24 hours, and serve as shots.

MOTOR OIL

- 1 oz Jagermeister
- ½ oz peppermint schnapps
- ½ oz cinnamon schnapps
- ½ oz coconut rum

Using a triple shot glass, pour the ingredients in the order above and serve.

NYMPHOMANIAC

- 1 oz spiced rum
- ½ oz peach schnapps
- ½ oz coconut rum

Shake the ingredients over ice, strain, and serve.

OATMEAL COOKIE

- ½ oz orange liqueur
- ½ oz butterscotch schnapps
- ½ oz Irish cream

Shake all of the ingredients over ice, strain into shot glasses, and serve.

OIL SPILL

- 1 oz cinnamon schnapps
- ½ oz Jagermeister

Layer the ingredients in the above order carefully and shoot.

Orgasm

- ½ oz peppermint schnapps
- ½ oz Irish cream

Pour the ingredients into the shot glass and serve.

Peppermint Patty

- 1 shot peppermint schnapps
- Squirt of chocolate syrup

Pour a shot of peppermint schnapps. Hold the schnapps in your mouth, squirt some chocolate syrup in, swish around, and swallow.

Polar Bear

- ½ oz crème de cacao
- ½ oz peppermint schnapps

Shake the ingredients over ice, strain into shot glasses, and serve.

ROASTED TOASTY

- ½ oz cinnamon schnapps
- ½ oz amaretto
- ½ oz coffee liqueur

Shake the ingredients over ice, strain into shot glass, and serve.

RED BARON

- ¾ oz peppermint liqueur
- ¼ oz cinnamon schnapps

Layer the ingredients in the above order carefully and serve.

RED HOT

- 1 ½ oz cinnamon schnapps
- Dash of Tabasco sauce

Pour the ingredients into a shot glass and serve.

RED SILK PANTIES

- ½ oz vodka
- ½ oz peach schnapps
- ½ oz cranberry juice

Shake the ingredients, strain, and serve.

RED, WHITE, AND BLUE

- 1/3 oz grenadine
- 1/3 oz peach schnapps
- 1/3 oz blue curacao

Layer the ingredients very carefully in the above order and serve.

REDHEAD'S NIPPLE

- 1 oz vanilla schnapps
- 1 oz Irish cream

Layer the ingredients in the above order carefully and serve.

REDHEADED SLUT

- 1 oz Jagermeister
- 1 oz peach schnapps
- 2 oz cranberry juice

Pour the ingredients into a shaker with ice. Shake, strain, and serve.

ROOT BEER FLOATIE

- ½ oz root beer schnapps
- ½ oz light cream

Layer the ingredients in the above order carefully and serve.

SANTA SHOT

- ½ oz grenadine
- ½ oz green crème de menthe
- ½ oz peppermint schnapps

Layer the ingredients in the above order carefully and serve.

S E X   O N   T H E   B E A C H

- 1 oz vodka
- 1 oz triple sec
- 1 oz apple schnapps
- 1 oz peach schnapps
- 1 oz Southern Comfort peach liqueur
- 2 ½ oz OJ
- 2 ½ oz 7-Up soda
- 1 tbsp grenadine syrup

Mix all of the ingredients in a pitcher of ice. Strain into a bottle and serve as shots.

S I L K   P A N T I E S

- 1 oz vodka
- ½ oz peach schnapps

Stir the ingredients in a glass, strain, and serve.

S M U R F   F A R T

- ½ oz blue curacao liqueur
- 1 oz blueberry schnapps
- Splash of cream

Shake over ice, strain into shot glasses, and serve.

SMURF ON THE RAG

- ½ oz peach schnapps
- ½ oz blue curacao liqueur
- 1 ½ oz whipped cream
- Couple drops grenadine syrup

Mix the schnapps and blue curacao in the shot glass. Top with whipped cream, add a couple drops of grenadine on top, and serve.

SMURF PISS

- 1 oz blue curacao liqueur
- 1 oz blackberry schnapps
- Splash pineapple juice
- Splash Sprite soda

Chill the ingredients, mix in a shot glass, and serve.

SNOWSHOE

- ¾ oz Wild Turkey Bourbon
- ¾ oz peppermint schnapps

Pour the ingredients into a shaker with ice. Shake, strain, and serve.

SOUTHERN BLUES

- ½ oz Southern Comfort peach liqueur
- ½ oz blueberry schnapps

Shake over ice, strain into a shot glass, and serve.

SQUISHED SMURF

- ½ oz peach schnapps
- ¼ oz Irish cream
- ¼ oz blue curacao liqueur
- Couple drops grenadine syrup

Layer the Irish cream on top of the peach schnapps. Dribble Blue Curacao over the top and it will curdle around the Irish cream. Drop in some grenadine around the shot glass and serve.

TOASTIE

- 1 ¼ oz amaretto
- 1/3 oz cinnamon schnapps

Pour the ingredients into a shot glass in the above order and serve.

WASHINGTON APPLE

- 1 oz Canadian Whiskey
- 1 oz sour apple schnapps
- 1 oz cranberry juice
- Apple slice

Pour the ingredients into a shaker with ice. Shake, strain, and serve with the apple slice as a garnish.

WILD THING

- ½ oz wildberry schnapps
- ½ oz bourbon
- ½ oz cranberry juice
- ½ oz sweet 'n sour

Pour the ingredients into a shaker with ice. Shake, strain, and serve.

Woo Woo

- ½ oz peach schnapps
- ½ oz vodka
- ½ oz cranberry juice

Shake the ingredients over ice, strain into shot glass, and serve.

TEQUILA

APOCALYPSE NOW

- 1/3 oz dry vermouth
- 1/3 oz Irish cream liqueur
- 1/3 oz tequila

Pour the ingredients into a shot glass and serve.

COLORADO RATTLESNAKE

- 1 ½ oz tequila
- 1 ½ oz tomato juice
- Dash of Tabasco sauceDash of black peppers

Pour the tequila, chilled, into a shot glass. Pour the tomato juice in another shot glass and add to it a dash of black peppers and a dash of Tabasco sauce. Shoot the tequila and it with the tomato juice chaser.

CROUCHING TIGER

- ½ oz SOHO Lychee Liqueur
- ½ oz %100 blue agave tequila

Shake the ingredients over ice, strain into shot glass, and serve.

CUCACARACHA

- ½ oz vodka
- ½ oz coffee liqueur
- ½ oz tequila
- Club soda

Mix in a large shot glass, top with the club soda, and serve.

EL VOCHO

- 1 ½ oz fine tequila
- 1 ½ oz pineapple juice
- 10 cilantro leaves
- 10 mint leaves
- Small slice of jalapeno

Pour the tequila in one shot glass. Blend all of the other ingredients and pour them in a separate shot glass. Take the tequila first and follow with the other shot as the chaser.

FIRE AND TORTURE

- 1 shot tequila
- 10 drops Tabasco sauce
- 5 splashes lime juice

Pour the tequila, followed by the Tabasco and lime juice, then serve.

FIRECRACKER

- ½ oz tequila
- ½ oz cinnamon schnapps
- ½ oz peppermint schnapps

Shake the ingredients over ice, strain into shot glass, and serve.

FOUR HORSEMEN

- ¼ oz Jim Beam bourbon whiskey
- ¼ oz Jack Daniel's whiskey
- ¼ oz Johnnie Walker Red Label Scotch whiskey
- ¼ oz Jose Cuervo Especial gold tequila

Pour into shot glass and serve.

HORNY BULL

- ¾ oz tequila
- ¾ oz rum

Pour into a shot glass and serve.

KAMIKAZE

- 1 oz tequila1 oz triple sec
- 1 oz lime juice

Pour into a shot glass and serve.

MEXICAN PRAIRE FIRE

- ¾ oz gold tequila
- ¼ Tabasco sauce

Pour tequila in the shot glass, top off with Tabasco sauce, and serve.

MEXICAN THREE WISE MEN

- 2/3 oz whiskey
- 2/3 oz bourbon whiskey
- 2/3 oz tequila

Mix all of the ingredients in a shot glass and serve.

NAZI TACO

- ½ oz Jagermeister
- ½ oz tequila
- ½ oz Tabasco sauce

Mix all of the ingredients in a shot glass and serve.

PIT BULL ON CRACK

- 1/3 oz tequila
- 1/3 oz Jagermeister
- 1/3 oz bourbon whiskey
- 1/3 oz 151 rum

Chill the ingredients, combine in a shot glass, and serve.

SANGRITA

- 1 shot tequila
- 1 oz fresh squeezed orange juice
- ¾ fresh squeezed lime juice
- ½ oz grenadine
- 3 dashes hot sauce
- slice of jalapeno

Pour the tequila in one shot glass. Shake the rest of the ingredients over ice, strain into another shot glass, and garnish with the jalapeno slice. Take the tequila shot with the sangrita mix as the chaser.

SOUL TAKER

- ½ oz vodka
- ½ oz tequila
- ½ oz amaretto

Mix together lightly in the shot glass and serve.

TEQUILA SLAMMER

- 1 oz tequila
- 1 oz ginger ale or lemon-lime soda

Pour the ingredients into a shot glass. Cover the glass with a napkin or just your hand. Slam the glass on the table and drink while it fizzes.

Z-28

- 1/3 oz green crème de menthe
- 1/3 oz banana liqueur
- 1/3 oz tequila

Layer the ingredients in the order above carefully and serve.

ZIPPER

- ½ oz Grand Marnier
- ½ oz tequila
- ½ oz Irish cream

Layer the ingredients in the above order carefully and serve.

VODKA

Apple Pie Shooter

- 2 shots apple juice
- 1 shot vodka
- Can of whipped cream
- Cinnamon

This shot is fun! The drinker is to sit in a chair, put their head back, and open their mouth. The pourer is to pour the apple juice, followed by the vodka shot into the drinker's mouth. Then the pourer sprays in some whipped cream and a tiny dash of cinnamon. The drinker finally sits up, mixes the drink in their mouth and swallows.

Apple Pie Shot

- ½ shot apple juice
- ½ shot vodka
- Dash of cinnamon

Pour the vodka and apple juice into the shot glass. Then put a dash of cinnamon on your tongue, put the shot in your mouth, shake, then swallow.

Ass

- ½ oz vodka
- ½ oz spearmint schnapps
- ½ oz sambuca

Pour the ingredients into a shot glass and serve.

Attitude Adjustment

- ½ oz Irish cream
- ½ oz root beer schnapps
- ½ oz Southern Comfort peach liqueur

Layer in the above order in a shot glass and serve.

Blue Lemonade

- 1 oz lemon vodka
- ½ oz blue curacao
- ¼ oz sweet and sour

Shake the ingredients over ice, strain into shot glass, and serve.

BLUE POLAR BEAR

- 1 oz vodka
- 1 oz chilled peppermint schnapps
- Crushed ice

Shake the vodka and peppermint schnapps until mixed. Add in the crushed ice for another light shaking and pour into shot glasses.

BRAIN ERASER

- 1 oz cinnamon schnapps
- 1 oz coffee liqueur
- 1 oz vodka

Layer in the above order in a large shot glass keeping everything separate. Slide a straw down the side of the glass carefully and suck from the bottom quickly!

CHINA WHITE

- ½ oz vodka
- ½ oz Irish cream
- ½ oz white crème de cacao

Shake everything over ice and strain into shot glasses.

C H O C O L A T E C A K E

- ¾ oz lemon vodka
- ½ oz hazelnut liqueur
- 1 lemon wedge

Mix in a shot glass and serve. Follow by sucking on a sugar-coated lemon wedge.

C U C A C A R A C H A

- ½ oz vodka
- ½ oz coffee liqueur
- ½ oz tequila
- Club soda

Mix in a large shot glass, top with the club soda, and serve.

C U M S C O R C H E R

- ½ oz butterscotch schnapps
- ½ oz vodka
- ½ oz coffee liqueur
- Dash Irish cream

Pour into a shot glass in the above order, slowly add the Irish cream last, and serve.

DEEP THROAT

- 1 oz vodka
- ½ oz Tia Maria
- Whipped cream

Layer the ingredients in the order above. Top with whipped cream and serve. Drink without using your hands!

FLAMING LEMON DROP

- 1 ½ oz lemon vodka
- Splash Galliano liqueur
- ½ slice lemon
- ¼ tsp sugar
- ¼ tsp Bacardi 151 rum

Fill the shot with lemon vodka and a splash of Galliano. Put the lemon slice flat on the shot glass and top it with sugar. Soak the sugar on the lemon slice with 151 and light it on fire. Blow out the flame when it is caramelized. Lick the sugar off the lemon, shoot the vodka, and bite the lemon.

F O R E S T   F I R E

- ¾ oz Everclear alcohol
- ¼ oz Tabasco sauce

Mix in a shot glass and serve.

F O U R T H   O F   J U L Y

- ½ oz grenadine
- ½ oz vodka
- ½ oz blue curacao

Layer the ingredients in the above order carefully then serve.

F U N K Y   B I T C H

- ½ oz coffee liqueur
- ½ oz vodka
- ½ oz Irish Cream
- ½ oz hazelnut liqueur

Shake the ingredients, strain, and serve.

HOOTER

- ¾ oz vodka
- ¾ oz amaretto

Pour the ingredients into a shot glass and serve.

HOT PANTS

- 1 oz peach schnapps
- ½ oz pepper vodka

Pour the ingredients into a shot glass and serve.

LEMON DROP

- 1 shot lemon vodka
- 1 slice lemon
- 1 tsp sugar

Pour the lemon vodka in the shot glass. Place the sugar on the lemon. Take the shot and bite the lemon as the chaser.

LEMON LIGHTNING

- ¾ oz Everclear alcohol
- ¾ oz lemon juice

Mix in the shot glass and place in the freezer for about half an hour to chill. Serve ice cold.

LEMON SHOT

- ½ oz Galliano liqueur
- ½ oz lemon vodka
- 151 rum
- Sugar
- 1 lemon wedge

Mix the lemon vodka and Galliano in the shot glass. Sprinkle sugar on the lemon wedge and place it on the shot glass. Pour 151 on the lemon wedge and glass. Light, let it burn for a moment, and blow it out. Take the shot and bite the lemon.

LIQUID COCAINE

- 1/3 oz orange liqueur
- 1/3 oz Southern Comfort peach liqueur
- 1/3 oz vodka
- 1/3 oz amaretto almond liqueur
- Splash pineapple juice

Shake everything over ice, strain, and serve in shot glasses.

MAGE'S FIRE

- 2 oz vodka
- 1 oz cinnamon schnapps
- 1 oz blue curacao liqueur

Mix the ingredients in a bottle, chill for 24 hours, and serve as shots.

MELON BALL

- ¼ oz melon liqueur
- ¼ oz pineapple juice
- ½ oz vodka

Pour the ingredients into a mixing glass with ice. Stir, strain, and serve.

M O O S E   F A R T

- 1 oz vodka
- 1 oz Canadian whiskey
- 1 oz coffee liqueur
- 1 oz Irish cream

Blend with ice until thick in consistency, pour into shot glasses, and serve.

N U T S ' N   B E R R I E S

- 2 oz lemon vodka
- 1 oz hazelnut liqueur
- 2 oz cranberry juice

Mix all of the ingredients and chill. After chilled, strain into shot glasses and serve.

P U R P L E   H O O T E R

- ½ oz vodka
- ½ oz raspberry liqueur
- Splash 7-Up soda

Shake the ingredients over ice, strain into shot glasses, and serve.

RED SILK PANTIES

- ½ oz vodka
- ½ oz peach schnapps
- ½ oz cranberry juice

Shake the ingredients, strain, and serve.

RUSSIAN QUAALUDE

- 1 oz hazelnut liqueur
- 1 oz Irish cream
- 1 oz vodka

Layer the ingredients in the above order and serve.

SEX ON THE BEACH

- 1 oz vodka
- 1 oz triple sec
- 1 oz apple schnapps
- 1 oz peach schnapps
- 1 oz Southern Comfort peach liqueur
- 2 ½ oz OJ
- 2 ½ oz 7-Up soda
- 1 tbsp grenadine syrup

Mix all of the ingredients in a pitcher of ice. Strain into a bottle and serve as shots.

S I L K P A N T I E S

- 1 oz vodka
- ½ oz peach schnapps

    Stir the ingredients in a glass, strain, and serve.

S I L V E R N I P P L E

- 1 oz sambuca
- 1 oz vodka

    Stir the ingredients in a glass, strain, and serve.

S N A K E B I T E

- ½ oz Green Chartreuse
- ½ oz vodka
- 2 drops Tabasco sauce

    Layer the ingredients carefully in the above order. Drop the Tabasco in so that the drops go to the bottom of the shot and serve.

SOUL TAKER

- ½ oz vodka
- ½ oz tequila
- ½ oz amaretto

Mix together lightly in the shot glass and serve.

STOPLIGHT

- 3 shots vodka
- Dash of cranberry juice
- Dash of orange juice
- Dash of melon liqueur

Pour the vodka into three shot glasses in a line on the bar. Pour a dash of cranberry juice in the first, orange juice in the second, and melon liqueur in the third. Now serve.

SUICIDE BLOND

- 1 oz vodka
- ½ oz pineapple juice
- Dash of triple sec
- Dash of lime juice

Shake the ingredients over ice, strain into shot glass, and serve.

W a t e r m e l o n

- 1 oz vodka
- 1 oz amaretto almond liqueur
- 1 oz Southern Comfort peach liqueur
- 1 oz OJ
- 1 oz pineapple juice
- Dash of grenadine syrup

Shake the ingredients over ice, strain into shot glasses, and serve.

W o o W o o

- ½ oz peach schnapps
- ½ oz vodka
- ½ oz cranberry juice

Shake the ingredients over ice, strain into shot glass, and serve.

Z a m b o d i a n

- 1 oz vodka
- 1 oz blackberry brandy
- 1 oz pineapple juice

Shake the ingredients over ice, strain into shot glasses, and serve.

WHISKEY

ALABAMA SLAMMER (WHISKEY)

- 1 oz amaretto almond liqueur
- 1 oz whiskey
- 1 oz OJ
- 1 oz crème de noyaux

Shake everything over ice, strain into shot glasses, and serve.

ANACONDA

- ¾ oz whiskey
- ¾ oz white sambuca

Shake the ingredients over ice, strain into shot glass, and serve.

AREOLA

- ½ oz peach schnapps
- ¼ oz Canadian whiskey
- ¼ oz sloe gin

Pour the ingredients in the above order into a shot glass and serve.

B OILERMAKER

- 1 shot whiskey
- 1 pint beer

Pour a shot of whiskey, drop it into the pint glass of beer, and chug.

C URTAIN C ALL

- ½ oz Jagermeister
- ½ oz melon liqueur
- ½ oz whiskey

Shake the ingredients over ice, strain into shot glass, and serve.

D EATH R OW

- ¾ oz whiskey
- ¾ oz 151 rum

Shake the ingredients over ice, strain into shot glass, and serve.

DUCK FART

- ½ oz whiskey
- ½ oz amaretto almond liqueur
- ½ oz Irish cream

Layer in the above order and serve.

EARTHQUAKE

- 1/3 oz Canadian whiskey
- 1/3 oz anise liqueur
- 1/3 oz gin

Shake the ingredients over ice, strain into shot glass, and serve.

FOUR HORSEMEN

- ¼ oz Jim Beam bourbon whiskey
- ¼ oz Jack Daniel's Tennessee whiskey
- ¼ oz Johnnie Walker Red Label Scotch whiskey
- ¼ oz Jose Cuervo Especial gold tequila

Pour into shot glass and serve.

GORILLA FART

- ½ oz 151 rum
- ½ oz bourbon whiskey

Pour into a shot glass and serve.

IRISH CAR BOMB

- ¾ pint Guinness
- ¾ oz Irish whiskey
- ¾ oz Irish cream

Pour the Irish cream in the shot glass and layer the whiskey on top. Pour the Guinness in a pint glass. Drop the shot into the pint glass and chug!

MEXICAN THREE WISE MEN

- ½ oz Jack Daniel's Tennessee whiskey
- ½ oz Jim Beam bourbon whiskey
- ½ oz Jose Cuervo Especial gold tequila

Mix all of the ingredients in a shot glass and serve.

M O O S E   F A R T

- 1 oz vodka
- 1 oz Canadian whiskey
- 1 oz coffee liqueur
- 1 oz Irish cream

Blend with ice until thick in consistency, pour into shot glasses, and serve.

P I C K E L B A C K

- 1 shot whiskey
- 1 shot pickle juice

Pour one shot of whiskey and another shot of pickle juice. Shoot the whiskey and follow with the shot of pickle juice.

P I T   B U L L   O N   C R A C K

- 1/3 oz tequila
- 1/3 oz Jagermeister
- 1/3 oz bourbon whiskey
- 1/3 oz 151 rum

Chill the ingredients, combine in a shot glass, and serve.

PRAIRE OYSTER

- 1 ½ oz bourbon
- 1 raw egg
- Dash of Tabasco sauce

Use a large shot glass and pour the bourbon in. Next, crack the egg and put it in raw. Add a dash of Tabasco and shoot.

RED ROYAL

- ¾ oz Canadian whiskey
- ¼ oz amaretto almond liqueur

Pour the ingredients into the shot glass in the above order and serve.

RED SNAPPER

- 1 oz Canadian whiskey
- 1 oz amaretto liqueur
- 2 oz cranberry juice

Pour into a shaker with ice. Shake, strain, and serve.

SNOWSHOE

- ¾ oz Wild Turkey Bourbon
- ¾ oz peppermint schnapps

Pour the ingredients into a shaker with ice. Shake, strain, and serve.

THREE WISE MEN

- ½ oz Johnnie Walker Scotch whiskey
- ½ oz Jim Beam bourbon whiskey
- ½ oz Jack Daniel's Tennessee whiskey

WASHINGTON APPLE

- 1 oz Canadian Whiskey
- 1 oz sour apple schnapps
- 1 oz cranberry juice
- Apple slice

Pour the ingredients into a shaker with ice. Shake, strain, and serve with the apple slice as a garnish.

WILD **T**HING

- ½ oz wildberry schnapps
- ½ oz bourbon
- ½ oz cranberry juice
- ½ oz sweet 'n sour

Pour the ingredients into a shaker with ice. Shake, strain, and serve.

Y 2 K

- ½ oz coffee liqueur
- 1 oz Canadian whiskey

Mix in a chilled shot glass and serve.

INDEX

www.ingramcontent.com/pod-product-compliance
Lightning Source LLC
Chambersburg PA
CBHW071227290326
41931CB00037B/2233